· MY · FIRST · LOOK · AT ·

Noises

Random House 🏠 New York

Hearing noises

There are noises all around us. Some
noises are loud. Some noises are soft.
We hear them with our ears.

A whisper is a soft noise.

This is a Dorling Kindersley Book
published by Random House, Inc.

Senior Editor Jane Yorke
Editor Charlotte Davies
Art Editor Toni Rann
Designer Heather Blackham
Photography Stephen Oliver,
Tim Ridley, Stephen Shott

Series Consultant Neil Morris
Models Laila Ayoubi, Lewis Blitz,
Mark Guildea, Miranda Hutcheon,
Bianca Irish-Barker, Yuksel Mustapha

Dorling Kindersley would like to thank Mr Wobbli Toys for carving the farm animals.

First American edition, 1991

Library of Congress Cataloging-in-Publication Data
My first look at noises.
   p. cm.
   Summary: Introduces the concept of noises through photographs of
musical instruments, noisy toys, animals making noise,
and other situations with sounds.
   ISBN 0-679-81161-3
   1. Noise – Juvenile literature. [1. Sound.] I. Random House (Firm)
II. Title: Noises.
   TD892.5.M93 1991
   534 – dc20
   90-8587 CIP AC

Manufactured in Italy 1 2 3 4 5 6 7 8 9 10

Reproduced by Bright Arts, Hong Kong
Printed and bound in Italy by L.E.G.O.

Animals also have ears.
They come in all shapes
and sizes.

This dog has floppy ears.

A rabbit has long,
pointed ears.

This mouse has tiny,
round ears.

An elephant has large, flapping ears.

Making noises

What loud noises can you make?

clap

stamp

shout

sing

Farm animal noises

What noises do these farm animals make?

Pigs say OINK!

Ducks say QUACK!

Cows say MOO!

Goats say MEH!

Sheep say BAA!

Horses say NEIGH!

Roosters say COCK-A-DOODLE-DOO!

Animal noises

bee

bird

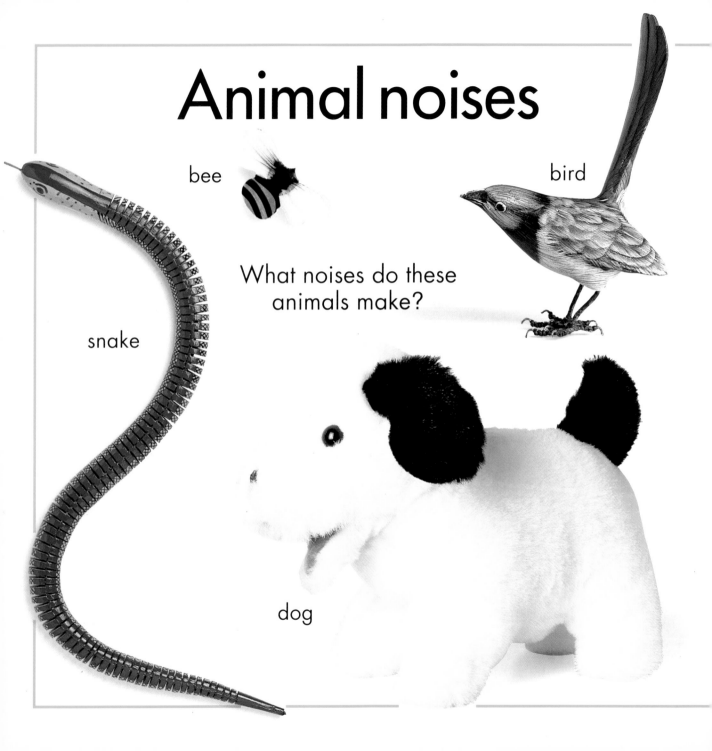

What noises do these animals make?

snake

dog

donkey

frog

cat

lion

Noisy toys

Do any of your toys make a noise?

wind-up toy

pull toy

music box

push toy

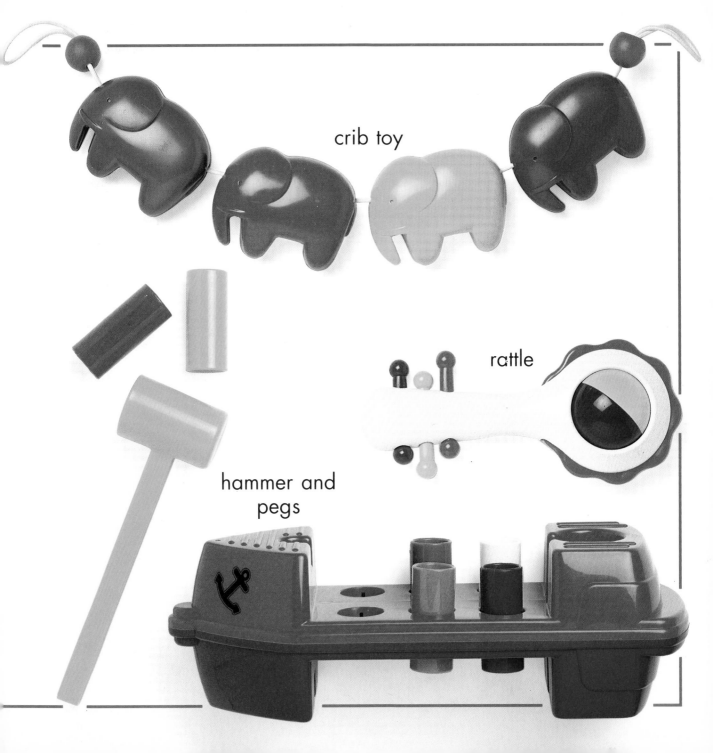

crib toy

rattle

hammer and
pegs

Musical sounds

You can make music with these instruments.

recorder

xylophone

drum

guitar

maracas

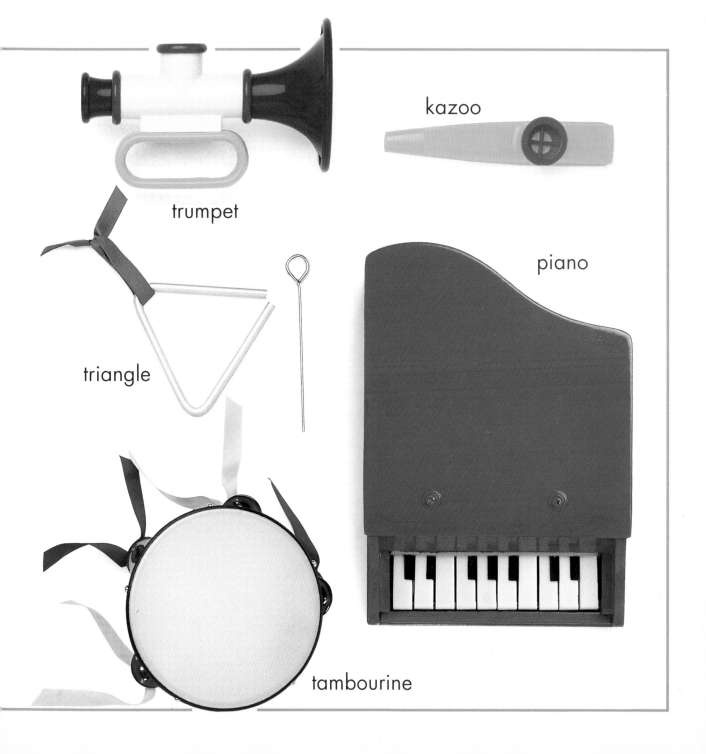

trumpet

kazoo

piano

triangle

tambourine

Things that go

fire engine

What noises do these
vehicles make?

motorcycle

train

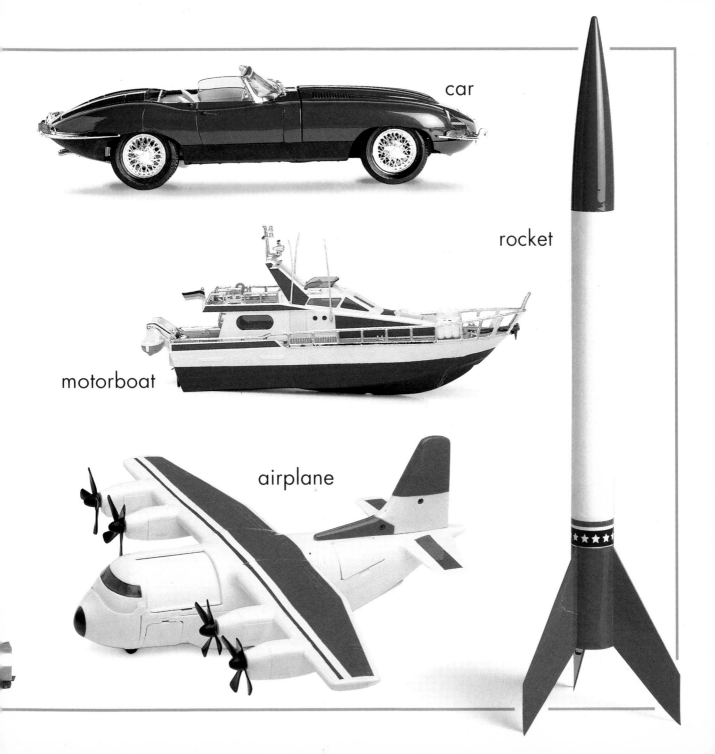

car

rocket

motorboat

airplane

Noises at home

What noises do you hear in your house?

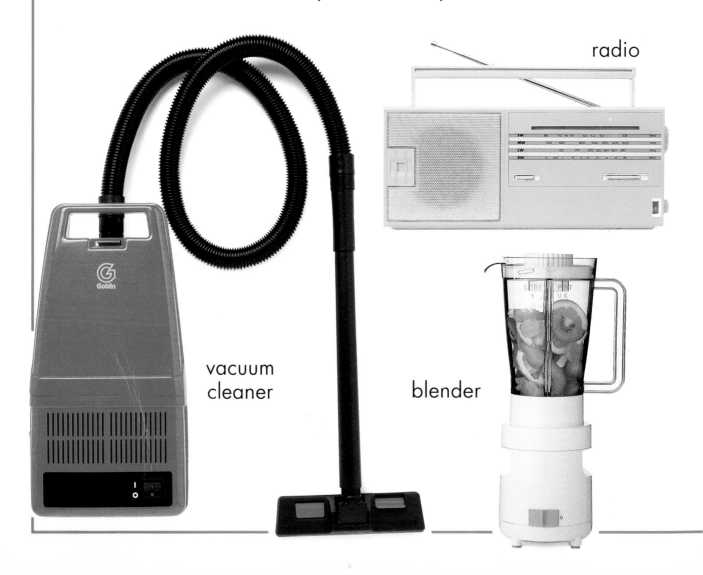

radio

vacuum
cleaner

blender

typewriter

blow-dryer

alarm clock

telephone

kettle